Law of Attraction

The Power In "I Am" "I Have" "I Believe"

100 Wealth Building Affirmations
Ignite The Power Within You
Achieve: Healing, Success, Wealth, Abundance and Prosperity

Living Word Publishing
4464 Seminole St.
Detroit, Mi 48214
www.livingwordpublishing.net

I0177662

Library of Congress Control Number: 2015944126

West-Gonzalez, Gwendolyn
   Law of Attraction: The Power In "I Am" "I Have" "I Believe"
      100 Wealth Building Affirmations

Summary "Teachings on the Law of Attraction to achieve health, joy, peace and wealth

   ISBN 978-0996372114 (trade pbk. : alk.paper) Philosophy/Spiritual Growth
/Mind/Body/Soul.

© 2015 by Healing Today Ministries
Grosse Pointe, Mi 48230
www.healingtoday.net

Printed in the United States of America. All rights reserved under International Copyright Law.

The information contained in this book is intended to be educational and not for diagnosis, prescription, or treatment of any health disorder whatsoever. This information should not replace consultation with a competent healthcare professional. The content of this book is intended to be used as an adjunct to a rational and responsible healthcare program prescribed by a health care practitioner. The author and publisher are in no way liable for any misuse of material.

7 6 5 4 3 2 1   1 2 3 4 5 6 7

LAW OF ATTRACTION

THE POWER IN "I AM" "I HAVE" "I BELIEVE"

100 WEALTH BUILDING AFFIRMATIONS

IGNITE THE POWER WITHIN YOU

ACHIEVE HEALING, SUCCESS, WEALTH, ABUNDANCE AND PROSPERITY

Copyright • Materials

TABLE OF CONTENT

LAW OF ATTRACTION

Over 100 Powerful Affirmations To Attract Abundance

PART ONE

THE POWER IN "I AM"

- I Am Debt Free
- I Am an Achiever
- I Am of Infinite Intellect
- I Am Living Abundantly
- I Am Grateful For My Abundance
- I Am Growing in Wealth and Wisdom
- I Am Passionate About Building Wealth
- I Am Absolutely Sure I Attract Abundance Daily
- I Am a Money Magnet and Money is Magnetic to Me
- I Am Vibrating and Attracting Everything Good in My Life
- And many, many more.....

Part Two
THE POWER IN "I HAVE"

- I Have Great Wealth
- I Have Self Worth
- I Have Protection
- I Have Unlimited Abundance
- I Have Creative Ability to Get Wealth
- I Have All My Needs Met Instantaneously
- I Have Love, Joy, Happiness, Peace and Prosperity
- I Have An Income That Is Increasing Higher and Higher
- I Have a Continuous Stream of Wealth Flowing in My Direction
- And many, many more.....

Part Three
THE POWER IN "I BELIEVE"

- I Believe In Love
- I Believe I Am Forgiven
- I Believe I Can Trust Again
- I Believe My Body is Healed
- I Believe Success is Attainable
- I Believe Wealth is My Birth Right
- I Believe I Can Live An Abundant Life
- I Believe I Have The Ability To Be Successful
- I Believe There Is Always A Divine Surplus of Money
- I Believe All Things Are Possible To Those Who Believe
- I Believe Money Is Forever Circulating Freely In My Life
- And many, many more...........

Part Four
Meditation Prayer

DEDICATION

This book is dedicated to:

ELOHIM (GOD)
THE CREATOR OF THE UNIVERSE

Who has loved me beyond my own comprehension and who have protected and blessed me beyond anything I could have ever imagined.

My Parents
Carl and Cassie West

There are no words that can express my appreciation for your unconditional love, commitment to rearing me in Christ and for being an example of what loyalty, confidence and trust means. You kept me protected from the world and ensured all my needs were met. You taught me what FAMILY means and gave me the mantle to pass these same values to my children. You gave me a moral compass in order for me to one day, discover a world rich with abundance. For that, I am grateful.

Many phrases you shared with me that equipped me for my divine quest. The ones that empowered me the most:

1. There is nothing you can not accomplish if you tell your mind you can do it.
2. You can do anything you put your mind to do.
3. Put God first in your life and you will never fail
4. Never burn your bridges.
5. Never give up, one day a door will open.
6. God is your power source, draw nigh to him and he will draw nigh to you.
7. Put God first in your life, everything else is second.

There is no other parent or family I would have rather attracted. I am tremendously happy I attracted you.

You are the love of my life!

"Greater love hath no man than this that a man lay down his life for his friends."

John 15:13

LAW OF ATTRACTION: DECLARATION

FIND INSPIRATION
THROUGH OUR GALLERIES

It is my hope that these daily affirmations draw you closer to understanding the power that is inside of you and the connection you, as a Spirit; have to the power of the Universe.

Whatever your need is at this season of your life, know that you deserve an abundant life filled with love, peace, happiness, health and wealth. God wants to enrich your life with everything you desire and more. The Universe is an infinite source of energy that is always circulating and vibrating. Every second of the day, a spirit is attracting what the universe is vibrating; whether it is peace for a confused mind, laughter for a sad soul, health for a diseased body, love for the brokenhearted, wealth for the persistent and the confident; the universe is always at work to will and to do what a Spirit wills.

In your quest to understand how to tap into the power of the universe through the Law of Attraction, the most important attraction you could ever activate or receive is the Spirit of Wisdom. There is The Spirit of Wisdom, The Spirit of Understanding, the Spirit of Knowledge and The Spirit of Might or Power - all are cornerstones to mastering all the Laws of the Universe. With these gifts you have an infinite intellect to discern the future and be victorious in every area of your life.   This infinite intellect is already in you, you just need to activate it.   The Word of God states, Wisdom is the principal thing; therefore get wisdom: and with all thy getting, get understanding (Proverbs 4:7).   The Spirit of Wisdom is the most important Spirit we can attract and is more profound as Spirits seek God.   As we seek God, He reveals "The Secret" to life, and our life's purpose.   If you truly want to know "The Secret" vigorously seek the eternal Spirit of God and you will be amazed at what the God of the Universe reveals to you.

"But seek ye first the kingdom of God, and his righteousness; and all these things shall be added unto you."

Matthew 6:33

LAW OF ATTRACTION

MASTER THE POWER WITHIN YOU

FIND INSPIRATION

This book is filled with powerful affirmations designed to empower - transforming whomever is willing to receive "The Secret" we call "The Law of Attraction" generate great wealth and healing.

Universal Laws, specifically the Law of Attraction is known to be the greatest secret discovered by many authors that dates back to the 16th century. It has been said that Isaac Newton, a physics scientist, stimulated the discovery of the Law of Attraction upon studying Albertus Magnus research of which applied the conception of 'affinity' to chemical systems. Fast forward to the 20th century when, from an interview conducted by Napoleon Hill to Billionaire, Andrew Carnegie shared the quantum physic phenomenon, of what is known today as "The Secret" with Hill upon which Carnegie, during a three hour interview with Hill, explained how anyone can obtain wealth and success. During the interview, Carnegie referred again and again to "The Secret" of prosperity and abundance. Not multiple secrets but "The Secret."

Be it known, we are all governed by a set of many Universal Laws. These Laws were created by the God head of the Spirits (us) for when the Spirits are transformed into the Earthly body the unity or Tri-part being (Spirit, Soul, Body) is able to work in harmony.

In order to ensure the Law of Attraction works in full effect, it is imperative that you know all the Laws and how they operate.

Although there are many Universal Laws, these 12 are the most profound.

12 Universal Laws for Mental Empowerment

——◆○◆◦╫╌ᕤ◦╫╌ᕫ┼╫╌┼ᕫ◦╫╌ᕤ┼╫╌◆○◆——

1. **The Law of Divine Oneness** - Everything is connected to something. What we think, say, do and believe will have a corresponding effect on others and the universe around us.

2. **Law of Vibration** - Everything in the Universe moves, vibrates and travels in circular patterns, the same principles of vibration in the physical world apply to our thoughts, feelings, desires and wills in the etheric body. Each sound, thing, and even thought has its own vibration frequency, unique unto itself.

3. **Law of Action** - Must be employed in order for us to manifest things on earth. We must engage in actions that supports our thoughts, dreams, emotions and words.

4. **Law of Correspondence** - This Universal Law states that the principles or laws of physics that explain the physical world; energy, light, vibration, and motion have their corresponding principles in the universe "as above, so below."

5. **Law of Cause and Effect** - The Law of Cause and Effect states that absolutely everything happens for a reason, nothing happens by chance or outside the Universal Laws.

All actions have consequences and produce specific results, as do all inactions. The choices we make are causes, whether they are conscious or unconscious, and will produce corresponding outcomes or effects. The Law works the same for everyone at all times. For every outcome or effect in one's life, there is a specific cause. For example, poor diet and exercise habits result in poor health, constant and uncontrolled spending results in debt and money worries, not putting effort into your key relationships results in poor relationships and all of the associated issues. In essence; "You Reap What You Sow."

6. **Law of Compensation** - This Universal Law works in harmony with the Law of Cause and Effect - sowing and reaping. It states that you are compensated for your efforts and for your contribution, whatever it is, whether large or small. This law also says that you can never be compensated in the long term for more than you put in. The income you earn today is your compensation for what you have done in the past. If you want to increase your compensation, you must increase the value of your contribution.

7. **Law of Attraction and Reaction**- Demonstrates how we create the things, events and people that come into our lives. This Law states our thoughts, feelings, words, and actions produce energies which, in turn attract like energies. Negative energies attract negative energies and positive energies attract positive energies.

8. **The Law of Perpetual Transmutation of Energy** - All humans have within them the power to change the conditions of their lives. Higher vibrations consume and transform lower ones; thus, each of us can change the energies in our lives by understanding the Universal Laws and applying the principles in such a way as to effect change.

9. **Law of Relativity** - Each person will receive a series of problems (tests / lessons) for the purpose of strengthening the light within each of these tests / lessons to be a challenge and remain connected to our hearts when proceeding to solve the problems. This law also teaches us to compare our problems to others problem into its proper perspective. No matter how bad we perceive our situation to be, there is always someone who is in a worse position. It is all relative.

10. **Law of Polarity** - Everything is on a continuum and has an opposite. We can suppress and transform undesirable thoughts by concentrating on the opposite pole. It is the law of mental vibrations.

11. **Law of Rhythm** - Everything vibrates and moves to certain rhythms. These rhythms establish seasons, cycles, stages of development, and patterns. Each cycle reflects the regularity of God's Universe. Masters of Law know how to rise above negative parts of a cycle by never getting to excited or allowing negative things to penetrate their consciousness.

12. **Law of Gender** - The law of gender manifests in all things as masculine and feminine. It is this law that governs what we know as creation. The law of gender manifests in the animal kingdom as sex. This law decrees everything in nature is both male and female. Both are required for life to exist.

These laws were created by God of the Universe, to assist us as Spirits co-exist in this 3 dimension world, we call Earth and to aid us in creating the life we desire while on this Earth plane. Once we made our transmission from the 4th dimension into the 3rd dimension and as young children, we was brain washed to believe what our parents or caregiver told us how we should think, talk or feel - because, as children we was unable to remember the life we lived in the 4th dimension - we believed all the non-sense that was fed to us.

Consequently, most foundational teachings we receive from adolescents to adulthood is negative thinking and as a result, most grow up living a life of anguish, heartache, disappointments, lack and just plain - defeat.

To truly know how to attract great health, abundant wealth, and true happiness is to understand and respect all the Universal Laws, then, and only then will you be on the road to mastering the Law of Attraction.

MASTERING THE LAW OF ATTRACTION TO GET WHAT YOU WANT

In observing people for the past few years, I have discovered that people find it very easy to conform to this world system. For example, the government makes it easy to apply for financial assistants to aid in paying for school tuition, getting a mortgage to pay for a house, vehicle loans, and even loans for home improvement projects. It is one's belief that this is "positive assistance" as oppose to manifesting what has already been created and freely taking possession of the thing you most desires.

Clearly, conforming to the world system of doubt, unbelief, fear and debt brings destruction. Everything you desire is already created. But it is up to you to manifest the thing that has already been created for you from the Universe. Due to many years of negative thinking; not thinking you deserve it, or that it wasn't meant for you, condemnation; you are not good enough and fear; fear of rejection; many turn to the government and not their creator, who created them and stored away everything they would ever need to survive on the Earth plane.

The God of the Universe has an infinite supply of everything you could ever want and need. The key to unlock that infinite supply is you must think it first, then you visualize it, once you visualize it, you believe it, once you believe it, you must speak it, and once you speak it; as God created the heaven and the earth with a spoken Word, it will manifest. It is just that easy.

When you change your thinking you change your circumstances. When you change your circumstances you change your life!

"Do not conform to this world but be ye transformed by the renewal of your mind"

Romans 12:2

———————

The Law of Attraction is one of the greatest laws in the universe. It simply states; if you think in negative terms you get negative results if you think in positive terms you achieve positive results. That is an astonishing fact that is the bases of the law of prosperity and success; in three words; believe and receive.

"If you can believe, all things are possible to him that believes."

Mark 9:23

A great author said "if you can believe it, you can achieve it." Believing is activated by thinking. If we can think it, we can achieve it. We become what we think about. And if this is the result, it stands to reason that a person that thinks and have concrete goals is always, without uncertainty, is going to reach it because that is what he strive and work hard to accomplish - naturally will succeed. Conversely, a man that has no goals with thoughts of confusion, anxiety, and worry will have no success because this is what he constantly thinks about. The person that thinks on negative thoughts, his life will be one of frustration, fear and defeat and his designation is that of a dead end.

So you may ask, how does the Law of Attraction really works? And why do we become what we think about?

I'm so glad you asked. I want to share a story that parallels how the mind works. The brain is a storage file that collects data that you verbally, as a programmer, program the mind to receive. The mind doesn't care what you put into it, it will accept anything you put into it and will return back what you put in. Let's reference the bible about the story of sowing and reaping. The bible uses the parable of the farmer that sows. In the bible the Word references the land. Let's use the land and refer it to your brain. It will return what you plant, but it doesn't care what you plant. The farmer has land and chooses to sow seed in that land. The land has great soil and is well fertilized. The land gives the farmer a choice; he may plant in that land whatever he chooses. The land doesn't care; it is up to the farmer to plant whatever he decides. I am comparing the human mind with the land because the mind, just as the land, doesn't care what you plant in it and will return what you plant. Again, the mind is like the land – it doesn't care what you choose to plant in it. This story, when meditated on, is a great awakening because it clearly explains that the brain will not reject anything; whether it is negative words or images. Just as the land will accept anything you plant. However, the end result is, what will it harvest? Will the brain harvest stinking thinking, thoughts of defeat and images that torment? Or will it harvest healing, wealth and abundance. At the end of the day, you are in control.

"It's time to switch from a scarcity consciousness to a prosperity consciousness."

Your Greatness Is Waiting!

HOW TO PROTECT YOURSELF AGAINST NEGATIVE INFLUENCES

To effectively protect yourself against negative influences, whether of your own making, or the result of others that bestow negativity around you, recognize that you have willpower. Ultimately, you make the final decision of who is in your inter-circle, what goes inside your ear gate, what appears in front of your eyes and what comes out of your mouth. Your goal is to block out any and ALL negativity by using your willpower to build a wall of immunity against negative influences. Your willpower stops negativity from building a nest in your mind and taking control over your thought process.

Unfortunately, it is a fact that humans are by nature, susceptible to all suggestions which harmonize with our weaknesses. Although, we all have weaknesses, we must identify them and turn our weaknesses into positive substances by changing our thought process. Know that both weaknesses and strengths are made of energy substances that have negative and positive affects, depending on how an individual is able to use that energy substance for their benefit.

There are six basic fears that determine how humans handle life situations and circumstances; as well as negative influences. By nature, humans are susceptible to all the six basic fears, as a result the mind generates signals of anxiety, fearfulness, uneasiness, nervousness, uncertainty and insecurity to cushion and embrace these fears of which humans begin to build habits as a normality not realizing the destructions this path will ultimately result in.

The Six Basic Fears

Many of you are familiar with Napoleon Hill, "Think and Grow Rich." In this classic book, Hill talks about the six basic fears most people are affected by and many fail in life due to not being aware that they are suffering from these fears. In chronological order, according to what statistics states most people exhibits includes:

1. The fear of poverty
2. The fear of criticism
3. The fear of ill health
4. The fear of loss of love
5. The fear of old age
6. The fear of death

The prevalence of these fears, as a curse to the world, runs in cycles. The onset of the fear of poverty stems and reaches a boiling point each time a war breaks out. Throughout history, it has been known that when a war breaks out there is no benefit. World War 11 caused the great depression with job lost, foreclosures, stock market crash and riots. Fast forward to 9/11 the same activities took place and the United States was in a worst condition again due to a war. With the onset of a war, people panic and as a result fear of poverty and death crystallizes. Fears are nothing more than states of mind. One's state of mind is subject to control and direction.

Fear paralyzes the faculty of reason, destroys the faculty of imagination, kills off self-reliance, undermines enthusiasm, discourages initiative, leads to uncertainty of purpose, encourages procrastination, wipes out enthusiasm and makes self control an impossibility.

To overcome these fears we must recognize that the brain receives and delivers everything we put in it. Fear is a result of indifference, indecisiveness, doubt, worry, over-cautiousness, procrastination, lack of self confidence and abilities; thus a person thinks and verbalizes negativity. Faith replaces fear, thus a person has the ability to reprogram their thought process with words and imagines that change their path from degenerations to regeneration. A person that has fear must recognize that fear is a negative influence that has a profound effect on emotions, willpower (goals), and thought process. And since negative influences are mostly taking residence in the subconscious mind, it is difficult to detect and can make one unaware. Fear destroys a person's ability to advance in life and many lose hope instead of taking back control of their life and demanding a life of abundance.

"The secret to the master mind is found wholly in the use of imagination."

Christian D. Larson (1874-1962)
New Thought Author

"God gave us a spirit not of fear but of power and love and self-control."

2 Timothy 1:7

Taking Back Your Life

The best way to protect yourself from negative influences is to deliberately seek the company of people who influence you to appreciate life and be thankful for the smallest gifts and gestures. Furthermore, don't ponder over the aches and pains your body is exhibited, and the heartache and disappointment someone did to you, as well as the lack of money you currently have, or where you stand right now in your current situation. Instead be happy and take joy for tomorrow is a new day that is filled with mercy and grace.

Laughter is a medicine and forgiveness of others heals all wombs, which opens the universe to bring you everything you desires.

The most important way you can protect yourself from negative influences is to be true to yourself. Know that you are a Spirit, that lives in a body and possess a soul (mind, will and emotions). You are first a Spirit that is made up of energy that attracts anything and everything you put out into the universe. Whatever you put out there, you will get back; whether good or bad.

Surround yourself with people that know who they are. Take control of your thought process and what you say, as a result you will live an abundant life!

"Keep your mind as much as you can from dwelling on your ailment. Think of strength and power and you will draw it to you. Think of health and you get it."

Prentice Mulford (1834-1891)
New Thought Author

HOW TO EFFECTIVELY USE AFFIRMATIONS

To be successful in using affirmations to get want you want, it all begins with understanding the subconscious mind.

The subconscious mind consists of a field of consciousness, in which every impulse of thought that reaches the objective mind through any of the five senses, is classified and recorded, and from which thoughts may be recalled or withdrawn as letters may be taken from a filing cabinet.

The brain receives, and files sense impressions or thoughts regardless of the content; whether images, sound and words. As the brain receives messages it is stored in the subconscious mind. These messages are in operation day and night and due to the extent of the content that is constantly being processed, the subconscious mind develops infinite intelligence beyond man's understanding. The subconscious mind cannot be controlled but it can be reprogrammed by managing what content is put in it and what visuals is seen through the eye gate and ear gate – from the music we listen to, the television and media programs we watch and the conversations we engage in with others. As we accept the fact that the things we say, think, and view affects the decisions we make in life, we come to the realization that the mind is the communication center that transmute thoughts into its physical and monetary equivalent. Meaning, whatever negative or positive activities we as humans participate in the same will manifest in the physical and in the monetary; resulting in poverty or wealth.

Know that the subconscious mind will not remain idle. It is always processing. If you fail to plant desires in your subconscious mind, it will feed upon thoughts of daily activities whether positive or negative and return what you do not want as oppose to what you want.

In Napoleon Hill's "Think and Grow Rich," Hill discusses 30 major causes of failure that is holding individuals back from achieving their desires or life goals.

Hill shares his analysis of several thousand men and women he studied over a period of time that tragically failed to succeed in life regardless of how hard they tried. In fact 98% of men and women he studied failed at successfully achieving life goals. As I list the thirty major causes of failure, evaluate yourself for the purpose of discovering how many of these causes - of - failure stand between you and your success.

1. **Unfavorable hereditary background** - There is very little one can do if born with a deficiency in brain power. This philosophy offers but one method of bridging this weakness and that is through resources, such as this book and others that empower individuals on their quest for success. This cause is the only of the thirty that may not be easily corrected by any individual.

2. **Lack of a well-defined purpose in life** - There is no hope of success for the person who does not have a central purpose, or definite goal to aim. Hill's analysis returned, ninety-eight out of every hundred of individuals he analyzed, had no such aim. It is determined that goal setting is the building block to accomplishing outcomes. Without clear defined goals, there is not direction. With no direction one is at a standstill, there is no movement thus they never reach their full potential.

3. **Lack of ambition to aim above mediocrity** - We offer no hope for the person who is so indifferent as not to want to get ahead in life, and who is not willing to pay the price. One must be enthusiastic with drive and ambition in order to be successful in receiving from the Universe.

4. **Insufficient education** - The lack of education is no excuse for failure. Experience has proven that the best-educated people are often those who are known as "self-made," or self-educated. It takes more than a college degree to make one a person of education. Any person who is educated is one who has learned to get whatever he wants in life without violating the rights of others. Education consists, not so much of knowledge, but of knowledge effectively and persistently applied. Men are paid, not merely for what they know, but more particularly for what they do with that which they know. There is a high percentage of millionaires and even billionaires without college degrees.

5. **Lack of self-discipline** - Discipline comes through self-control. This means that one must control all negative qualities. Before you can control conditions, you must first control yourself. Self –mastery is the hardest job you will ever tackle. If you do not conquer self, you will be conquered by self. You may see both at the same time your best friend and your enemy, by stepping in front of a mirror.

6. **Ill health** - No person may enjoy outstanding success without good health. Many of the causes of ill health are subject to mastery and control. These include:

   1. Overeating of foods not conductive to health.
   2. Wrong habits of thought; giving expression to negatives.
   3. Wrong use of and over indulgence in sex.
   4. Lack of proper physical exercise.
   5. An inadequate supply of fresh air, due to improper breathing.

7. **Unfavorable environmental influences during childhood** - "As the twig is bent, so shall the tree grow" Most people who have criminal tendencies acquire them as the result of a bad environment and improper associates during childhood. This can have a profound effect in a positive and negative way, depending on the strength of the person's ability to not allow pass experiences interfere with living a successful life; nonetheless, few overcome these obstacles.

8. **Procrastination** - This is one of the most common causes of failure. The phase "Old Man Procrastination" stands within the shadow of every human being waiting for his opportunity to destroy one's chances of success. Most of us go through life as failures because we are waiting for the "time to be right" to start doing something worthwhile. Do not wait! The time will never be "just right." Start where you currently are today and work with whatever tools you may have at your command; as a result, better tools and resources will be found as you go along. Success just doesn't happen. It is a process that is actively working as you are passionately seeking and doing.

9. **Lack of persistence** - Most of us are good "starters" but poor "finishers" of everything we begin. Moreover, people are prone to give up at the first signs of defeat. When this happens, fear chokes the person into believing that success is inevitable thus failure dominates. Failure cannot cope with persistence. An individual that is persistent and doesn't allow challenging situations to rain supreme, success becomes attainable!

10. **Negative personality** - There is no hope of success for the person who repels people through a negative personality. Success comes through the application of power, and power is attained through the cooperative efforts of the other people. A negative personality will not induce cooperation, thus it decreases your power to attract anything positive in the Universe.

11. **Lack of controlled sexual urge** - Sex energy is the most powerful of all the stimuli, which move people into action. Because it is the most powerful of the emotions, it must be controlled, transformed, and converted into proper channels. Most people misinterpret the urge for sexual activity to mean I need gratification from the opposite sex when in actuality the urge you are feeling is the energy to transform this passion you are feeling into activities that produce valuable resources, such as business ownership to build wealth for the betterment of mankind.

12. **Uncontrolled desire for "something for nothing"** -The gambling instinct drives millions of people to failure. Many people spend an excessive amount of time in casinos gambling on luck. There is a misuse or misunderstanding of how the Universe works in attracting money. Spending your life's savings, your entire paycheck, retirement and your children's college savings is not the way. Additionally, many people depend on the Government to be their lifetime resource. Both the Government and the Casinos was not design to make you rich, let alone successful. The Law of the Universe, specifically the Law of Attraction says put out nothing you receive nothing, put out something of substance; that is, love, peace, joy, you receive the same.

13. **Lack of a strong power of decision** - People who succeed reach decisions promptly. They are great decision makers. People who fail, reach decisions, if at all, very slowly and change them frequently, and quickly.

Decision making and procrastination are twin brothers. Where one is found, the other is usually found also. Kill off this pair before they completely "hog –tie" you to the treadmill of failure. To make better decisions, know what you want, have definite goals, and do what you are passionate about.

14. **One or more of the six basic fears** - 1.The fear of poverty, 2. The fear of criticism, 3. The fear of ill health, 4. The fear of loss of love, 5. The fear of old age, and 6. The fear of death must be realized before you can advance in life. Once you conquer your fear (s) you can conquer your world.

15. **Poor selection of a mate in marriage** - This is the most common cause of failure. The relationship of marriage brings people intimately into contact. Unless this relationship is harmonious, failure is likely to follow. Moreover, it will be a form of failure that is marked by misery and unhappiness, destroying all signs of ambition and creativity.

16. **Over-caution** -The person, who takes no chances, generally has to take whatever is left when others are through choosing. Over-caution is as bad as under-caution. Both are extremes to be guarded against. Life itself is filled with the element of chance. Being over-cautions is derived by fear. If you allow fear to be the corporate behind your decision to not succeed in life, that of which you fear will control you.

17. **<u>Wrong selection of associates in business</u>** -This is one of the most common causes of failure in business. Although you may have had a great product or service to provide to the marketplace, the selection of business partners and employees can have a profound effect on the success or failure of your new business venture. Use great care to select a business partner and employees who will be an inspiration to others, and who is knowledgeable with a successful track record. We emulate those with whom we associate most closely. Select partners and employees who are worth emulating.

18. **<u>Superstition and prejudice</u>** - Superstition is a form of fear. It is also a sign of ignorance. People who succeed have an open mind and are afraid of nothing.

19. **<u>Wrong selection of a vocation</u>** - No man can succeed in a line of endeavor which he does not like. To increase the success rate select an occupation into which brings joy and ignite the power within you.

20. **<u>Lack of concentration of effort</u>** - The "Jack-of-all-trades" seldom is good at any. Concentrate all of your efforts on one definite chief aim.

21. **<u>The habit of indiscriminate spending</u>** - The spend-thrift cannot succeed, mainly because he stands in fear of poverty. Systematic saving is in your power. Putting aside a definite percentage of your income decreases your chances of failure. Money in the bank gives one a

very safe foundation. Without money, one must take what one is offered and be glad to get it.

22. **Lack of enthusiasm** - Without enthusiasm one cannot be convincing. Moreover, enthusiasm is contagious and the person, who has it, is generally welcome in any group of people.

23. **Intolerance** -The person with a "closed" mind on any subject seldom gets ahead. Intolerance means that one has stopped acquiring knowledge. The most damaging forms of intolerance are those connected with religious, racial, and political differences of opinion.

24. **Intemperance** - The most damaging forms of intemperance are connected with eating, strong drink, and extreme sexual activities. Overindulgence in any of these is fatal to success. Every activity must be done in moderation. A balanced life brings great rewards.

25. **Inability to cooperate with others** - More people lose their positions and their big opportunities in life because of this fault, than all other reasons combined. It is a fault which no well-informed business man or leader will tolerate. In order to be successful you must develop business contacts by networking with other business owners. Being a "people person" is essential to your success or failures.

26. **Possession of power that was not acquired through self-effort** - This failure is individuals of sons and daughters of

wealthy men and others who inherit money of which they did not earn. Power in the hands of one who did not acquire it gradually, is often fatal to success. Quick riches are more dangerous than poverty. This is through the study of several who received a large amount of money from winnings or inherited money from a rich uncle. These individuals either splurged all their winnings and inheritance due to the lack of self control or lost their lives.

27. **Intentional dishonesty** - There is no substitute for honesty. One may be temporarily dishonest by force of circumstances over which one has no control, without permanent damage. But, there is no hope for the person who is dishonest by choice. Sooner or later his deeds will catch up with him and he will pay by loss of reputation, and perhaps even loss of liberty.

28. **Egotism and vanity** - These qualities serve as red lights which warn others to keep away. They are fatal to success.

29. **Guessing instead of thinking (assuming)** - Most people are too indifferent or lazy to acquire facts with which to think accurately. They prefer to act on "opinions" created by guesswork or snap-judgments. Be resourceful and research the facts before jumping headlong into any venture to avoid failure.

30. **Lack of Faith in one's own abilities** - Although we have covered reasons why people fail, fear and a lack of faith

and confidents in self are major reasons people fail or just don't try at all.

Upon exploring the corporate behind the reason (s) people fail at success or just don't try at all opens the door for misfortune for their entire family generation. This is called "generational curse." I found that when I evaluate a person's family tree, one or several of these causes for failure exist. In order for a person to break the chain of these activities and turn these failures into success, the person must take a personal inventory of themselves.

A self-analysis is essential to determine if a person is repeating past mistakes and if they are advancing in life. When you know who you are, you can identify what makes you, you. Every person is unique in their own way, but there are traits that are passed down by our ancestors that must be identified in order to rewire the brain to think differently, from a positive standpoint. When there are activities that is causing one to fail based on negative characteristics and activities that was programmed in ones subconscious mind as young child, it is possible for the subconscious mind to be reprogrammed.

Since the subconscious mind draws upon the forces of infinite intelligence and is very powerful in transmitting all activities of which is controlling thought and translating thought into a belief system; thus, it is imperative that affirmations is precise, clear, and short.

With these affirmations, remember that the Law of Attraction works with the Law of Harmony which is that of our Spirits we harmonize and vibrate with everything – seen and unseen. If we are not harmonizing love, joy, peace; then the Law of Attraction will not work to your benefit. You must harmonize with the Fruit of the Spirits before you can attract healing, success and wealth. One cannot develop a wealth conscious until he has mastered the spirit of love, the spirit of joy, the spirit of kindness, and the spirit of peace. To receive the Law of Harmony, pray to the God of the Universe for divine harmony and He will give it to you freely. Practice the Law of Harmony daily. Once you have actively mastered living the Law of Harmony, then you can practice the Law of Attraction through affirmations. Nature insists on you having a balance and being the salt in the Earth that you may bring the Earth flavor like salt is flavor to food. Without salt there is no flavor, thus everything is bland. You are important to the universe, find your quest for living and use your creativity and power wisely.

Remember you are living in a subjective and objective world, therefore you must not neglect the spiritual food such as peace of mind, love, beauty of harmony, joy and laughter.

"The fruit of the Spirit is love, joy, peace, forbearance, kindness, goodness, faithfulness, gentleness and self-control. Against such things there is no greater law."

Galatians 5:22-23

THE FORCE OF LOVE TO ACTIVATE WEALTH

"Love is an element which though physically unseen is as real as air or water. It is an active, living, moving force...it moves in waves and currents like those of the ocean."

Prentice Mulford (1834-1891)
New Thought Author

The Universal love or the Agape love is deeper then the affectionate love given to your family, friends and favorite things. Most people give love based on conditions; you love me, therefore I love you. The Universe loves unconditionally and He sees no color, creed, national origin, or sexual preference. Love is the act of doing. It is the positive force of life and the only verb that causes everything good to manifest good. The Spirit of Love is the only positive energy that, within it, activates dunamis (dynamite) power to attract instant results, faster than any other acts of kindness.

Nature's great powers, like gravity and electromagnetism, are invisible to our senses, but their power is indisputable. Likewise, the force of love is invisible to us, but its power is in fact far greater than any of nature's powers. The evidence of its power can be seen everywhere in the world: without love, there is no life.

Take a moment to think about it: What would the world be like without love? First of all, you would not exist; without love you could not have been born. None of your family and friends would have been born either. In fact, there would not have been a single human on the planet. If the force of love ceased today, the entire human race would decrease and eventually die out.

Everything you want to be, do, or have comes from love. As a father, you wake up every morning for work to provide for your family because you love them and want the best for them. As a mother, you are motivated by love to cook healthy meals, clean the house, wash clothes, and sing sweet melodies to your children. The positive force of love propels you to work, play, dance, teach, learn, laugh, inspire and have compassion for others. Without love you are like a stone statue. The positive force of love can create anything good, increase the good things, and change anything negative in your life. The Spirit of love gives you the power over your health, your wealth, your career, your relationships, and everything imaginable in your life. And that "Power" is inside of everyone. The answer is, if everyone in the world activated the "Power" of love, more people will be healthy, wealthy, and liberated.

The Spirit of Love is the Law of Attraction. Charles Haanel states, "The law of attraction or the law of love...they are one and the same." The force of attraction is the force of love! Attraction is love. When you feel an attraction to your favorite food, you are feeling love for that food; without attraction you would not feel anything. All food would be the same to you. Without attraction you would not be attracted to another person, a particular city, house, car, sport, job, music, clothes, or anything, because it's through the force of attraction that you feel love.

The Law of Attraction is the law of love, and it is the all-powerful law that keeps everything in harmony. It is operating in everything and through everything in the Universe. Most importantly, it is the Spirit that is operating in your life!

The universal term for the Law of Attraction simply states, like attracts like, which means whatever you give out in life is exactly what you will attract back to yourself.

Every action of *giving* creates an opposite action of *receiving* and what you receive is always equal to what you have given. It is the Law of Attraction!

Give positivity, you receive back a full life of positivity; give negativity, you receive back a full life of negativity. Now you may ask, how do you give positivity or negativity? You give positivity and negativity through your words, actions, thoughts and feelings.

At any moment, you are giving positive words, actions, thoughts and feeling or negative words, actions, thoughts and feelings; and whether they are positive or negative determines what you receive back in your life. All the people, circumstances, and events that make up every moment of your life are being attracted back to you through the words, actions, thoughts and feelings you're giving out. Life doesn't just happen to you; you receive everything in your life based on what you have given out.

As a Spirit, the force of our energy vibrates and magnetizes everything. For example, when your actions, words, feelings and thoughts are negative you will vibrate and magnetize negative circumstances. Here is a great scenario that was shared with me by a friend. He awaken one morning and as soon as his foot touch the floor, his first thought was, as he looked out the window, shaking his head, it is going to be a bad day, because it is raining and then the words came out of his mouth, "Oh no…it is raining; it is going to be a horrible day." All of a sudden, he could not find his rubber boots and umbrella, upon leaving the house, he approached his car to discover he had a flat tire, and as he struggled, trying to unscrew the bolts on the rim of the tire, the bolts had become rusted. Finally, he headed off to work and drove right into a major traffic jam. Upon arriving to work late, he was called into the boss's office to be assigned to a major project that will pull an all nighters, and his list went on and on.

We react to circumstances by first seeing, thinking, feeling then speaking. The manifestation of the circumstance is determined by what we see, think, feel and say. When you see a circumstance you automatically think on it, whether good or bad, then you feel bad or good, then you say what we think the outcome will be, whether good or bad. As a result you magnetize what you think and said. The thought and the words are now out of your mouth and in the universe - bring back exactly what you thought and said.

Now let's relate this process to wealth. The Law says, give out positive thoughts, feeling and words about money and you will magnetize positive circumstances, people, and events that bring more money to you. I have a close friend that is an affirmation queen and stands by reciting affirmations on a daily bases to attract clients and money. She is always sharing how she increased her business and bank account by using the Law of Attraction. With great excitement, she proclaims how she starts her day with an affirmation of "it's a great day to become a millionaire." With this statement early in the morning, she is setting the tone for a day of expectancy. She is creating her life with thoughts and words. To add to this, if she feels like a millionaire in a matter of time, she will become a millionaire.

As surely as you think, say and feel - the law of attraction is responding to you. It doesn't matter whether your thoughts and feelings are good or bad, you are giving them out and they will return to you as automatically and precisely as an echo returns the same words you send out.

It is not too late to change the way you think, the words you speak and the way you feel. If you change your thinking and speech patterns now, in a matter of time you will change your life to receive over and beyond everything you could ever imagine.

"Every moment of your life is infinitely creative and the Universe is endlessly bountiful. Just put forth a clear enough request, and everything your heart desires must come to you."

Shakti Gawain (1948-)
Author

OVER 100 POWERFUL AFFIRMATIONS TO ATTRACT ABUNDANCE

PART ONE

THE POWER IN "I AM"

FIND INSPIRATION
THROUGH OUR GALLERIES

"Whatever the mind can conceive, and believe, the mind can achieve."

Napoleon Hill

(Repeat 3 times)

✦ I am a Spirit

✦ I am a Spirit   ✦I am a Spirit

✦ I am a powerful energy source
  ✦ I am a powerful energy source
    ✦ I am a powerful energy source

✦ I am a bright light that illuminates power
  ✦ I am a bright light that illuminates power
    ✦ I am a bright light that illuminates power

✷ I am made in the image and likeness of God
✷I am made in the image and likeness of God
✷ I am made in the image and likeness of God

✷ I am of infinite intelligence
✷ I am of infinite intelligence
✷ I am of infinite intelligence

✷ I am creative   ✷I am Loved
   ✷ I am creative   ✷I am Loved
     ✷ I am creative   ✷I am Loved

✷ I am honored   ✷I am favored
   ✷ I am honored   ✷I am favored
     ✷ I am honored   ✷I am favored

     ✷ I am beautiful
✷ I am beautiful   ✷I am beautiful

✷ I am healthy   ✷I am a winner
  ✷ I am healthy   ✷I am a winner
    ✷ I am healthy   ✷I am a winner

✷ I am an achiever   ✷I am beloved
  ✷ I am an achiever ✷I am beloved
✷ I am an achiever   ✷I am beloved

  ✷ I am healed   ✷I am held in high esteem
✷ I am healed   ✷I am held in high esteem
  ✷ I am healed   ✷I am held in high esteem

---

* I am passionate   *I am focused
   * I am passionate   *I am focused
      * I am passionate   *I am focused

---

      * I am helpful to others
* I am helpful to others   *I am helpful to others

---

    * I am a giver   *I am a leader
    * I am a giver   *I am a leader
    * I am a giver   *I am a leader

---

*I am wealthy   *I am successful
   *I am wealthy   *I am successful
*I am wealthy   *I am successful

---

*   I am like God; therefore I have the power to get wealth
*   I am like God; therefore I have the power to get wealth
*   I am like God; therefore I have the power to get wealth

---

   * I am a visionary   *I am forgiven
* I am a visionary   *I am forgiven
     * I am a visionary   *I am forgiven

---

   * I am loyal   *I am debt free
     * I am loyal   *I am debt free
   * I am loyal   *I am debt free

---

*   I am happy   *I am a learner
*   I am happy   *I am a learner
*   I am happy   *I am a learner

---

* I am advancing, growing, and moving forward financially
* I am advancing, growing, and moving forward financially
* I am advancing, growing, and moving forward financially

* I am a nurturing parent
* I am a nurturing parent
* I am a nurturing parent

* I am a loving spouse
* I am a loving spouse
* I am a loving spouse

* I am a retainer of information
* I am a retainer of information
* I am a retainer of information

* I am worthy of great success
* I am worthy of great success
* I am worthy of great success

* I am victorious
* I am victorious
* I am victorious

* I am courageous
* I am courageous
* I am courageous

* I am bold
* I am bold
* I am bold

* I am prospering everyday
* I am prospering everyday
* I am prospering everyday

✸   I am growing in wealth and wisdom
✸   I am growing in wealth and wisdom
✸   I am growing in wealth and wisdom

✸   I am a money magnet and money is magnetic to me!
✸   I am a money magnet and money is magnetic to me!
✸   I am a money magnet and money is magnetic to me!

✸   I am living abundantly
✸   I am living abundantly
✸   I am living abundantly

✸ I am absolutely sure I attract abundance daily
✸   I am absolutely sure I attract abundance daily
✸ I am absolutely sure I attract abundance daily

✸   I am grateful for my abundance
✸   I am grateful for my abundance
✸   I am grateful for my abundance

✸ I am passionate about building wealth
✸ I am passionate about building wealth
✸ I am passionate about building wealth

✸   I am vibrating and attracting everything good in my life!
✸   I am vibrating and attracting everything good in my life!
✸   I am vibrating and attracting everything good in my life!

Great Job!

"Keep on asking, and you will receive what you ask for. Keep on seeking and you will find. Keep on knocking, and the door will be opened to you."

Matthew 7:7 (NLT)

PART TWO

THE POWER IN "I HAVE"

FIND INSPIRATION

"I press on toward the goal to win the (supreme and heavenly) prize to which God in Christ Jesus is calling us upward."

Philippians 3: 14 (AMP)

(Repeat 3 times)

✚ I have wisdom to make right decisions for my life
✚ I have wisdom to make right decisions for my life
✚ I have wisdom to make right decisions for my life

✚ I have passion	✚ I have self worth
✚ I have passion	✚ I have self worth
✚ I have passion	✚ I have self worth

✚ I have hope	✚ I have protection
✚ I have hope	✚ I have protection
✚ I have hope	✚ I have protection

✚ I have confidence   ✚ I have success
✚ I have confidence   ✚ I have success
✚ I have confidence   ✚ I have success

✚ I have doubled my income
✚ I have doubled my income
✚ I have doubled my income

✚ I have great wealth
✚ I have great wealth   ✚I have great wealth

✚ I have abundance in all of its' form
✚ I have abundance in all of its' form
✚ I have abundance in all of its' form

✚ I have great listening skills
✚ I have great listening skills
✚ I have great listening skills

✚ I have a sharp mind
✚ I have a sharp mind
✚ I have a sharp mind

✚ I have comprehension
✚ I have comprehension
✚ I have comprehension

✚ I have 20/20 vision
✚ I have 20/20 vision
✚ I have 20/20 vision

✚ I have crisp hearing
✚ I have crisp hearing   ✚ I have crisp hearing

✚ I have extraordinary memory
✚ I have extraordinary memory
✚ I have extraordinary memory

✚ I have peace, love and a sound mind
✚ I have peace, love and a sound mind
✚ I have peace, love and a sound mind

✚ I have joy   ✚ I have happiness
✚ I have joy   ✚ I have happiness
✚ I have joy   ✚ I have happiness

✚ I have forgiven myself
✚ I have forgiven myself
✚ I have forgiven myself

✚ I have so much promise
✚ I have so much promise
✚ I have so much promise

✚ I have more money coming in then going out
✚ I have more money coming in then going out
✚ I have more money coming in then going out

✚ I believe everyday my wealth is multiplying
✚ I believe everyday my wealth is multiplying
✚ I believe everyday my wealth is multiplying

✚ I have unexpected money coming to me daily

✚ I have unexpected money coming to me daily

✚ I have unexpected money coming to me daily

✚ I have victory over my circumstances

✚ I have victory over my circumstances

✚ I have victory over my circumstances

✚ I have many loving friends

✚ I have many loving friends

✚ I have many loving friends

✚ I have supernatural increase of clients daily

✚ I have supernatural increase of clients daily

✚ I have supernatural increase of clients daily

✚ I have the manifestation of riches in my life

✚ I have the manifestation of riches in my life

✚ I have the manifestation of riches in my life

✚ I have great potential to fulfill my divine destiny

✚ I have great potential to fulfill my divine destiny

✚ I have great potential to fulfill my divine destiny

✚ I have a loving and caring family

✚ I have a loving and caring family

✚ I have a loving and caring family

✚ I have obedient, respectable and loving children

✚ I have obedient, respectable and loving children

✚ I have obedient, respectable and loving children

✚ I have a continuous stream of wealth flowing in my direction
✚ I have a continuous stream of wealth flowing in my direction
✚ I have a continuous stream of wealth flowing in my direction

---

✚ I have unlimited abundance
✚ I have unlimited abundance
✚ I have unlimited abundance

✚ I have an income that increases higher and higher
✚ I have an income that increases higher and higher
✚ I have an income that increases higher and higher

✚ I have all my needs met instantaneously
✚ I have all my needs met instantaneously
✚ I have all my needs met instantaneously

✚ I have creative ability to get wealth
✚ I have creative ability to get wealth
✚ I have creative ability to get wealth

✚ I have love, joy, happiness, peace and prosperity
✚ I have love, joy, happiness, peace and prosperity
✚ I have love, joy, happiness, peace and prosperity

✚ Abundance and prosperity is my birth right!
✚ Abundance and prosperity is my birth right!
✚ Abundance and prosperity is my birth right!

Great Job!

"Destiny is no matter of chance. It is a matter of choice."

William Jennings Bryan (1860-1925)
United States Political Leader

PART THREE

THE POWER IN "I BELIEVE"

FIND INSPIRATION
THROUGH OUR GALLERIES

"God has not given me a spirit of fear and timidity, but of power, love and self –discipline."

2 Timothy 1:7 (NLT)

(Repeat 3 times)

★ I believe I am a tri-part being: spirit, soul, body
★ I believe I am a tri-part being: spirit, soul, body
★ I believe I am a tri-part being: spirit, soul, body

★ I believe I am in control of my destiny
★ I believe I am in control of my destiny
★ I believe I am in control of my destiny

★ I believe I am victorious ★I believe I am loved
★ I believe I am victorious ★I believe I am loved
★ I believe I am victorious ★I believe I am loved

★I believe the Universe wants me to prosper
★ I believe the Universe wants me to prosper
★ I believe the Universe wants me to prosper

★I believe I attract positive energy
★ I believe I attract positive energy
★ I believe I attract positive energy

★ I believe positive energy is attracted to me
★ I believe positive energy is attracted to me
★ I believe positive energy is attracted to me

★ I believe I am connected to the Universe
★ I believe I am connected to the Universe
★ I believe I am connected to the Universe

★ I believe my vibration is vibrating everything good
★ I believe my vibration is vibrating everything good
★ I believe my vibration is vibrating everything good

★I believe wealth is my birth right
★ I believe wealth is my birth right
★ I believe wealth is my birth right

★ I believe my dreams are fulfilled
★ I believe my dreams are fulfilled
★ I believe my dreams are fulfilled

★ I believe all my needs are met
★ I believe all my needs are met
★ I believe all my needs are met

★ I believe in love ★ I believe my children are safe
★ I believe in love ★I believe my children are safe
★I believe in love ★I believe my children are safe

★ I believe my spouse is loyal to me
★ I believe my spouse is loyal to me
★ I believe my spouse is loyal to me

★ I believe I can live an abundant life
★ I believe I can live an abundant life
★ I believe I can live an abundant life

★ I believe I can buy a new home
★ I believe I can buy a new home
★ I believe I can buy a new home

★ I believe I can be a business owner
★ I believe I can be a business owner
★ I believe I can be a business owner

★ I believe I can buy a car
★ I believe I can buy a car
★ I believe I can buy a car

★ I believe I have a loving family
    ★ I believe I have a loving family
        ★ I believe I have a loving family

        ★ I believe my friendships are loyal
    ★ I believe my friendships are loyal
★ I believe my friendships are loyal

    ★ I believe I can love again
        ★ I believe I can love again
          ★ I believe I can love again

    ★ I believe I will get married
    ★ I believe I will get married
  ★ I believe I will get married

    ★ I believe I am forgiven
★I believe I am forgiven   ★ I believe I am forgiven

    ★ I believe I can trust again
  ★ I believe I can trust again
    ★ I believe I can trust again

      ★ I believe my future is bright
    ★ I believe my future is bright
  ★ I believe my future is bright

★ I believe my body is healed
    ★ I believe my body is healed
      ★ I believe my body is healed

★ I believe money is forever circulating freely in my life
★ I believe money is forever circulating freely in my life
★ I believe money is forever circulating freely in my life

★ I believe there is always a divine surplus of money
★ I believe there is always a divine surplus of money
★ I believe there is always a divine surplus of money

★ I believe success is attainable
★ I believe success is attainable
★ I believe success is attainable

★ I believe I can finish whatever I start
★ I believe I can finish whatever I start
★ I believe I can finish whatever I start

★ I believe I can do anything
★ I believe I can do anything   ★ I believe I can do anything

---

★ I believe I have the ability to be successful
★ I believe I have the ability to be successful
★ I believe I have the ability to be successful

★ I believe all things are possible to those who believe!
★ I believe all things are possible to those who believe!
★ I believe all things are possible to those who believe!

Great Job!

"All you can possibly need or desire is already yours. Call your desires into being by imaging and feeling your wish fulfilled."

Neville Goddard (1905-1972)
New Thought Author

PART FOUR

MEDITATION PRAYER

FIND INSPIRATION
THROUGH OUR GALLERIES

Within each of us there is the ability to feel images, to see what is beyond sight, to touch reality that can hardly be captured in mere words. Yet, it is often through words that we communicate those images, those sights, that reality.

Meditation is one of the best tools we have to counter the brain's negativity bias, release accumulated stress, foster positive experiences and intentions, and enjoy the peace of present moment awareness. A large body of research has established that having a regular meditation practice produces tangible benefits for mental and physical health, while vibrating positive signals to attract positive results for a more enriched life.

When starting a meditation regimen, set aside a time and place of quietness. Do not allow any distractions to interfere with this time of meditation and oneness with self. The best time is preferably at night right before you resign for bed.

You can set the tone with soft lighting and soft nature music or binaural beats. You can sit upright in a lazy boy reclining chair or lay comfortably in bed, with your eyes closed. Put yourself in a place of oneness with your mind, body and soul. Relax your body and allow your subconscious mind to willingly accept the suggestive affirmations you recite or listen to if you have recorded your meditations on a CD.

Begin with a breathing technique before speaking or listening to your meditation on a CD. Take deep breaths, inhaling inward and outward slowly. Allow your thoughts and the stresses of the day drift away with each breath – inhaling inward and outward slowly. Allow your muscles to relax. Feel your body relax with each deep, slow breath. It is the nature of the human body to enjoy relaxation. (repeat the breathing technique 3-4 times until your body is completely relaxed into oneness with your subconscious mind)

As your body drifts into a relaxed state, focus on the words you say and allow it to penetrate your subconscious mind.

I am one with the Universe and the Universe gives me health, wealth, joy, peace, protection and great abundance. I am grateful for my abundance. I am channeling positive energy to attract money, and those that have the tools and ability to help me succeed. As a co-creator, I am creating my future to attract business ideas. Within me, I have everything I need to accomplish my divine destiny. I give love therefore I attract love. I am willing to share my talents with others therefore I attract those that are willingly open to share their talents and ideas with me. It is a truth that I am a money magnet and was born wealthy, therefore I am wealthy. I am confident and deserve the abundance that the Universe has released to me.

Money never stops flowing to me; it flows continuously like a river. I am wondrously perfect and express the love that is within me. All the energy and emotions I attract are beautiful and harmonious in every way and I am grateful for all that the Universe has given me.

Well Done!

"Keep on asking, and you will receive what you ask for. Keep on seeking, and you will find. Keep on knocking, and the door will be opened to you."

Matthew 7:7 (NLT)

"For as a man thinketh in his heart, so is he."

Proverb 23:7 (NLT)

ABOUT
HEALING AND WEALTH INSTITUTE

The Healing and Wealth Institute was developed by the universal laws that whole up this Earth plane, specifically principles of the Law of Attraction.

The institutions purpose is to help all come into the realization of who they are, as a Spirit and how to operate in the Earth to live a life of abundance while fulfilling their divine destiny.

It is associated with Healing Today Broadcast Ministries, which is a prophetic healing ministry broadcasted weekly on your local cable stations.

To learn more about the Healing and Wealth Institute and studies on Law of Attraction, do visit our website at www.healingtoday.net.

Materials

As a student of the Law of Attraction it is important to equip yourself by adding valuable resources to your library that will empower you to attract everything you desire.

Feel free to email us:
livingwordministries@netzero.net
or
www.healingtoday.net

Be sure to send your testimonies once you receive the manifestation of what you have been seeking.

Donations

We depend on donations. Please visit our website at www.healingtoday.net to partner and support the ministry of Jesus Christ.

Order Copies for Bulk Retail Distribution
www.livingwordpublishing.net

The Healing and Wealth Institute is dedicated to promoting Health and Wealth to all that want to live an abundant life. Please be sure to visit our website often for more empowering resources and new releases.

Coming Soon!

Mental Empowerment: Unlock the Secret to Abundance
Strategies to a Rich Fulfilled Life

July 2015

This powerful book was inspired by Best Seller; Think Yourself to Health, Wealth, & Happiness and The Power of Your Subconscious Mind - is sure to transform your life for a more prosperous outcome.

Order Your Copy Today!

www.amazon.com
or
www.healingtoday.net

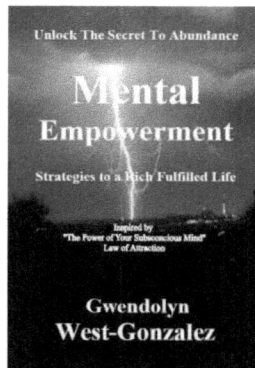

www.ingramcontent.com/pod-product-compliance
Lightning Source LLC
Chambersburg PA
CBHW071637040426
42452CB00009B/1671